Slither, Slide, Hop, and Run

By Katharine Kenah

School Specialty. Publishing

D1051336

Library of Congress Cataloging-in-Publication Data is on file with the publisher.

Send all inquiries to:
School Specialty Publishing
8720 Orion Place
Columbus, OH 43240-2111

ISBN 0-7696-4272-1

1 2 3 4 5 6 7 8 9 10 PHXBK 10 09 08 07 06 05

12-26-17

Table of Contents

Fly

A bird can **fly**!
It **moves** through the air with wings.

A bird flaps its wings.
It pushes down on the air
to lift up its body.
A bird's wings are covered
with feathers.
These feathers are light and strong.
They help the wings move air.

Slither

A snake can **slither**!
It wiggles from side to side
on the ground.

A snake has many ribs.
These ribs are covered with muscles.
The muscles tighten and relax
in waves.
This helps a snake move forward.
A snake pushes against plants
and rocks to move, too.

Hop

A kangaroo can **hop**!
It makes short leaps into the air.

A kangaroo has big, strong back feet.
It uses its back feet to hop.
When a kangaroo hops,
its back feet push off the ground.
Both feet rise into the air together.

Run

A horse can **run**!
Its legs move forward
and backward very quickly.

A horse has long legs and
strong muscles.
Each horse's step, or stride,
goes a long way.
A horse wears horseshoes on its feet.
These are hard metal plates that
protect a horse's feet.

Slide

A snail can **slide**!
It moves slowly along the ground.

A snail has a soft body
inside its hard shell.
Its body gives off a sticky slime.
A snail moves by sliding along
on this slime.

Crawl

A spider can **crawl**!
It creeps forward with its legs.

A spider has eight legs.
Most spiders have tiny claws
on the end of each leg.
Each claw has hairs around it.
The claws and hairs help a spider
hold onto things as it moves.

Swim

A dolphin can **swim**!
It moves gently through the water.

A dolphin's tail has
two flat flukes.
The flukes are very strong.
A dolphin does not swim like a fish.
A fish swims by moving its tail
side to side.
A dolphin swims by moving its tail
up and down.

Hang

A sloth can **hang**!
It holds onto a tree and hangs
below it.

A sloth has long claws
on its arms and legs.
The claws are like hooks.
They hold onto a tree branch tightly.
A sloth spends most of its life
hanging upside-down!

Glide

A bat can **glide**!
It flies smoothly through the air.

A bat does not have feathers.
Its wings are really long fingers
covered with skin.
Sometimes, a bat folds up its wings.
It walks on its small, weak legs.

Dig

A dog can **dig**!
It uses its paws to move dirt.

A dog runs and plays.
It also digs in the dirt.
A dog has strong legs and paws.
Each of its paws is covered
with sharp claws.
A dog uses its claws to dig
into the ground.

Climb

A raccoon can **climb**!
It moves up and down by using its feet.

A raccoon climbs almost everything!
Its front and back feet work like hands.
Each foot has long toes
and long, strong claws.
These claws help a raccoon grip things.

Waddle

A penguin can **waddle**!
It rocks from side to side as it walks.

A penguin waddles because
it has a tall body and short legs.
It looks like a slow way to move,
but a penguin can waddle
as fast as a person walks!

You Move, Too!

How do you move?
You move by changing
the position of your body.

Your body is full of muscles.
These muscles work together
to help you move.
You can slither, hop, run, slide,
crawl, swim, hang, glide, dig,
climb, and waddle!

Vocabulary

climb–to move up and down using hands and feet. *My neighbor saw four raccoons climb her tree.*

crawl–to creep forward with the body low. *Did you see the spider crawl across your chair?*

dig–to move dirt from one place to another. *My dog digs holes in our backyard.*

fly–to move through the air with wings. *Birds fly south for the winter.*

glide–to move smoothly without starting and stopping. *Bats glide across the sky at night.*

hang–to hold onto something above. *The sloth hangs from the tree as it sleeps.*

hop–a short leap into the air. *Kangaroos hop about at night, looking for food.*

move–to change the position of the body. *It feels good to move after sitting a long time.*

run–to move legs quickly over the ground. *The racehorses run around the track.*

slide–to move in a smooth line without stopping. *The snail slides along the ground.*

slither–to move side to side over the ground. *The snake slithered through the garden.*

swim–to move in water. *Dolphins swim in oceans around the world.*

waddle–to rock from side to side while walking. *Penguins can waddle on ice without falling down!*

Think About It!

1. Can you think of ways that animals move differently from the ones used in the story?

2. How do feathers help a bird fly?

3. Why do penguins waddle?

4. When a kangaroo hops, how many of its feet leave the ground at one time?

5. What is a fluke? How does it help an animal move?

The Story and You!

1. If you had to move like an animal, which animal would you choose to move like? Why?

2. Name six different things that move, not including people or animals.

3. Imagine that you could suddenly fly. How would your life be different?

4. How do the parts of your body help you to move?

5. If you had to either hop or crawl to school, which movement would you choose? Which do you think would take longer?